YOUR SEXUAL HEALTH™

URINARY TRACT INFECTIONS

SUSAN HENNEBERG

ROSEN
PUBLISHING®

New York

Published in 2016 by The Rosen Publishing Group, Inc.
29 East 21st Street, New York, NY 10010

Copyright © 2016 by The Rosen Publishing Group, Inc.

First Edition

Library of Congress Cataloging-in-Publication Data

Henneberg, Susan.
Urinary tract infections/Susan Henneberg.—First edition.
     pages cm.— (Your sexual health)
Includes bibliographical references and index.
ISBN 978-1-4994-6082-7 (library bound)—ISBN 978-1-4994-6083-4 (pbk.)—ISBN 978-1-4994-6182-4 (6-pack)
1. Urinary tract infections—Popular works. I. Title.
RC901.8.H46 2016
616.6—dc23

                                                                    2014042050

Manufactured in the United States of America

CONTENTS

INTRODUCTION

Maybe you have felt the telltale symptoms of a urinary tract infection (UTI): the constant urge to pee, the burning when you do, the ache in your pelvic region. Or maybe you have given excuses to cover the UTI of a friend. "Oh, she drank a lot of coffee this morning," you say about her many trips to the restroom. UTIs can make you miserable. Once you get one, you know you never want to get another one. Knowing how to treat and prevent UTIs will help you stay healthy, especially if you are sexually active.

According to the National Kidney and Urologic Diseases Information Clearinghouse (NKUDIC), UTIs are the second most common type of infection in the body. Almost 50 percent of women get a UTI at some point in their lives. Some women get recurrent UTIs, two or three each year. A urinary tract infection is one of the most common reasons why teens, especially girls, visit the doctor. Guys can get UTIs as well. UTIs in men are rare, but when they happen they are often more serious than those in women.

Almost half the women in the United States will get an infection in their urinary tracts during their lifetimes. Luckily, they are easily treated.

UTIs are sometimes called the honeymoon disease or honeymoon cystitis. Some teens think that getting a UTI is a giveaway that a girl has become sexually active. What is the connection? Having sex is the most common way that harmful bacteria finds its way into a girl's urethra. It is not the only way. Because of women's anatomy, UTIs can happen to young women for a variety of reasons.

UTIs need to be treated by a doctor. They are quickly diagnosed with a urine sample and are usually easily treated with antibiotics. Modern technology has increased the doctors' ability to prescribe the right antibiotic for the particular strain of bacteria a patient may have. Until the infection clears up, sufferers need to rest, drink lots of fluids, and take over-the-counter pain medications. If a UTI is not treated, it can become a kidney infection, a more serious disease.

In its early stages, a UTI can be embarrassing. If it happens to you, you will have to stay close to a bathroom. You may have to explain your condition to school nurses, teachers, and coaches. You will have to reassure family, friends, and sexual partners that you are not contagious. If you choose, you can take advantage of this opportunity to educate those close to you about this type of infection. In any case, you will find that learning as much as you can about UTIs will speed your recovery and prevent you from getting another one.

CHAPTER ONE

What Is a Urinary Tract Infection?

What is the purpose of the urinary tract? You know the equation. If you drink, you pee. However, urine is more than the water you drank after your daily run. The body makes urine to get rid of the waste and extra water that you don't need. Urine is also a way for your body to regulate the amount of water in your body. Excess water is eliminated as urine. The urine travels through the urinary tract on its way out of your body. The urinary tract is a pathway that includes several important organs.

You have two kidneys that serve identical purposes. They are bean-shaped organs that filter waste substances from the blood and produce urine to get rid of them. Without kidneys, the substances would build up as toxins. The ureters are thin tubes that take urine from the kidneys to the bladder. The bladder holds the urine until it's time to go to the bathroom. The urethra is the tube that carries urine from the bladder out of the body.

THE DIFFERENCE BETWEEN MALE AND FEMALE URINARY SYSTEMS

The basic organs and purpose of male and female urinary systems are the same. However, there are some important differences. Girls have short urethras. The urethra's only purpose is to take urine from the bladder out of the body. The opening of the urethra is close to the anus, the outlet for the digestive system. The urethra is also close to the vagina. The position of the opening of the urethra close to the anus and vagina makes it easier for bacteria to travel these short distances. That is

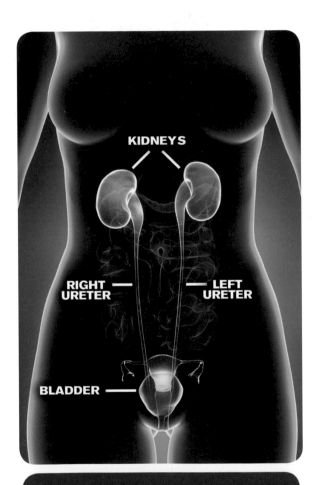

KIDNEYS

RIGHT URETER

LEFT URETER

BLADDER

Women get more UTIs than men because it is easier for bacteria to travel from the anus and vagina up to the urethra.

why females get more infections in their urinary tracts than males.

Boys share their urinary system with their reproductive system. Their urethras are longer than those of girls. The male urethra extends through the penis. It is also responsible for ejaculating semen through the penis. Because of the long male urethra and its distance from the anus, it is harder for bacteria to get into the urinary tract. Males get a lot fewer UTIs than females.

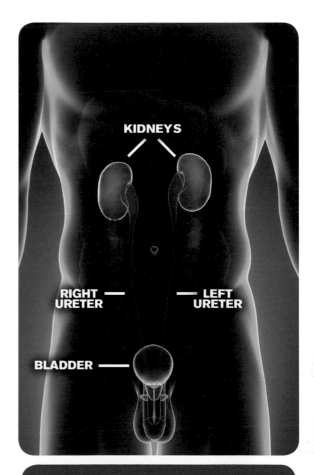

KIDNEYS

RIGHT URETER — — LEFT URETER

BLADDER —

The male urethra's length and its position in the body protect men from most, but not all, UTIs. UTIs in men can be serious.

WHAT CAUSES A UTI?

The first time you get a UTI you will be wondering what is going on. Your bladder will constantly feel as if you need to pee immediately. However, when you get to the bathroom, only a small amount passes out, and it burns. After you describe your symptoms to a doctor, he or she will immediately know the problem. A UTI is one of the most common infections that young women get.

The doctor will probably ask you for a urine sample. In addition to the normal waste products usually filtered by the kidneys, your urine will also contain bacteria. Bacteria are

E. COLI

E. coli is the shortened name of a bacteria called *Escherichia coli*. *E. coli* lives in your intestines. Most types are harmless. Some types, however, can make you sick. You can get *E. coli* infections by eating spoiled or contaminated food. One type of *E. coli* causes traveler's diarrhea, called that because many travelers pick up bacteria that their bodies aren't used to by eating or drinking unclean substances. Some *E. coli* is dangerous and can cause kidney failure and even death. You can avoid getting sick from *E. coli* by washing your hands frequently with soap. Make sure you wash fruits and vegetables before you eat them. Cook food, especially meat, to the temperature recommended by the U.S. Centers for Disease Control and Prevention (CDC). Avoid contaminating food in your kitchen by washing all surfaces with soap.

microbes so small they can be seen only with a microscope. This bacteria, usually *E. coli*, has traveled up through the urethra and infected the bladder, causing a bladder infection, or cystitis. The bladder wall is irritated by the bacteria, causing pain. Bacteria can also infect the urethra, resulting in urethritis. It can infect the kidney, which causes pyelonephritis, a more serious disease. If you have back pain, high fever, and vomiting, you might have a kidney infection.

THE CONNECTION BETWEEN UTIs AND SEXUAL ACTIVITY

UTIs are sometimes called the honeymoon disease or honeymoon cystitis. Brides who have a lot of sex during their honeymoons create conditions favorable to bladder infections. There are many other reasons why some women get bladder infections and why some women get more infections than others. Female biology is to blame.

There are a few ways that bacteria can get introduced into the urethra. If a girl wipes after a bowel movement from back to front, small amounts of stool can be pushed to the urethra. The stool contains bacteria from the digestive system. Having sex can push bacteria from the vaginal area into the urethral opening. Couples who switch between anal and vaginal sex without cleaning in between can cause bits of feces to get near the urethra. This is why young women who are sexually active can often get UTIs. These types of infections are not contagious, so you can't catch a UTI from someone else.

Using a spermicide, such as in contraceptive creams, jellies, sponges, and foams, during sex can increase your chances of getting a UTI. The purpose of spermicides is to kill sperm during sex to prevent pregnancy. Spermicides can also kill off naturally occurring good bacteria that protect against invading bad bacteria. The invading bacteria are able to establish colonies and create infection.

Women who use diaphragms are at risk for UTIs. They usually use them with spermicidal jelly or cream. Another reason diaphragms may cause UTIs is that they push up against the urethra, making it harder to fully empty the bladder. The urine that is left can grow bacteria.

The spermicide used with diaphragms can also kill off the protective bacteria that naturally occurs in women's vaginas.

ADDITIONAL GROUPS AT RISK

One group of people who are more at risk

Diabetics need to check their glucose levels frequently. High levels of glucose can put diabetics at risk for more UTIs than nondiabetics.

for UTIs are those who are diabetic. Diabetes is a disease in which people have high levels of sugar, or glucose, in their blood. Type 1 diabetes occurs when the body doesn't produce enough insulin. Insulin is necessary to use and store the glucose that comes from food. Those with type 2 diabetes don't respond well to the insulin their bodies make.

Diabetics get UTIs at a higher rate than the rest of the population. There are several reasons why. One reason is that people with diabetes have more glucose in their urine. The glucose provides food for the invading bacteria to multiply. Another reason is that some diabetics have nerve damage in their bladders. Their bladders don't contract enough to completely empty when they urinate. Urine left in the bladder for a long time provides an environment where bacteria can grow. A third reason is that diabetes can lead to reduced circulation of the blood. This reduces the ability of white blood cells, which fight infection, to get to the bacteria and kill it.

People with abnormalities in their urinary tracts can often get more UTIs. For instance, some people develop pouches in their bladders called diverticula. A pouch like this allows urine to collect inside, instead of being voided during urination. The stagnant urine is a breeding ground for bacteria. Other people have a ureter or urethra that is too narrow. This abnormality might prevent urine from leaving the kidney or bladder in the normal way. If urine stays too long in the urinary tract, an infection might develop.

People who have spinal cord injuries (SPI) are at higher risk for UTIs than the general population. These injuries often require the patient to use a catheter to urinate. A catheter is a thin tube that is inserted into the urethra. It allows urine to flow from the bladder into a drainage bag. The catheter can be another way that bacteria are introduced into the bladder. The catheter needs to be kept clean and replaced frequently to prevent a UTI.

Some people are more at risk than others. Those whose immune systems are compromised by other conditions can be more susceptible to UTIs. Pregnant women are also susceptible because of hormonal changes in the body. A growing uterus can press on the bladder, preventing it from completely emptying.

A urinary tract infection is painful and uncomfortable. Half of all women can expect to experience one over their lifetimes. Everyone can learn common sense strategies to prevent UTIs and treat the ones they do get efficiently and effectively.

CHAPTER TWO

How Do I Treat My UTI?

"I am 15 and I just had sex for the first time . . . I'm almost positive I have a UTI, but there is no way I'm telling my mom and getting medical attention for it, she can't know I've had sex . . . HELP!"

This is a letter published on May 2, 2013, on the teen sex education website Scarleteen. The sex education expert who answered the letter had some very important advice. She reinforced what the letter writer already knew. The teen needed to get to a doctor immediately. UTIs rarely go away by themselves. Instead, untreated infections just get worse.

Many teens are afraid that getting a UTI is a red flag announcing to the world that they are sexually active. Though having sex is a major cause of UTIs, it is not the only one. The expert on the website had several suggestions for the teen. The girl can admit to her mom that she has a UTI and not disclose her sexual activity. The girl may have the option to visit a school clinic for treatment. She may also be able to secretly visit a clinic where she can pay on her own for treatment. Or, she may convince her medical practitioner to allow her a confidential appointment without a parent present. Ultimately, the expert reminded the teen that if she is mature enough to be sexually active, she needs to be mature enough to take responsibility for her health—and her relationship with her parents.

THE SYMPTOMS

One of the first symptoms of a UTI is a frequent urge to urinate. But when you run to the bathroom to pee, only a little comes out. Not only is this annoying, it can be painful. You might feel a burning sensation. Both the urge and burning sensation are caused by an inflamed and irritated bladder and urethra. This inflammation causes the muscles of the bladder to spasm, which produces the urge to pee. The urge and burning can vary in severity. Some people feel burning and pain all the time. Some report only a feeling of pressure.

The color of the urine can also be a clue as to whether you have a UTI. Usually urine is light yellow. If yours is dark yellow,

Urine color can be an indication of a UTI. Cloudy urine indicates the presence of white blood cells, which are fighting a possible infection.

this may be an indication that you are dehy-drated and need to drink more water. Cloudy urine is a symptom of a UTI. The cloudiness is caused by an abundance of white blood cells, which are there to fight infection. The infection may also cause blood to leak into the bladder. The blood may give your urine a pink tinge.

There may be other symptoms that point to a bladder infection. A body fighting an infection may result in a fever. Even a rise of a degree or two can slow bacteria's growth. When the body's temperature rises, it gets confused and gener-ates even more heat by contracting and relaxing muscles. This may cause you to shiver with the chills. Some people feel nausea, which may lead to vomiting. Some may feel an ache in the lower abdomen.

WHAT SHOULD I DO IF I THINK I HAVE A UTI?

While a UTI is not a serious illness if promptly treated, it can be disruptive. If you are like most teens, you lead a very busy life. In addition to school, you may have sports, clubs, a job, and homework. You will not feel like doing any of these activities with a UTI. Bacterial infections need to be treated with prescription antibiotics. As soon as you feel any of the symptoms of a UTI, you need to

A UTI cannot be self-treated. A health professional is needed to prescribe the necessary antibiotics to treat the infection.

see a health professional. An untreated UTI can turn into a more serious kidney infection. If you can't get into your doctor's office, you'll need to visit an urgent care center or hospital emergency room.

The first step at the doctor's office or clinic is to diagnose the UTI. You will be asked for a clean-catch urine specimen. The doctor or nurse will ask you to go into a bathroom and clean your genital area with an antiseptic disposable wipe. Then you need to pee into a sterile cup. Your urine will be tested to look for white blood cells, red blood cells, and bacteria. If any of these are present, the doctor will prescribe an antibiotic. You will need to fill the prescription at a pharmacy as soon as possible.

Once you start taking the antibiotic, a series of pills taken several times a day, you should start feeling better. Some patients will be given a three- to five-day course of antibiotics. Others might need to take the pills for seven to ten days. You need to take every pill, even if you start feeling better before the pills run out. You need to completely kill off the bacteria or the infection will come back. If you are feeling a lot of pain, the doctor can pre-scribe a medication to relieve the muscle spasms and pain in your bladder. This medication will turn your urine a bright orange color. It will usually make you feel more comfortable within a few hours. If, after a few days, you are not feeling better, you need to call your doctor and ask him or her what to do.

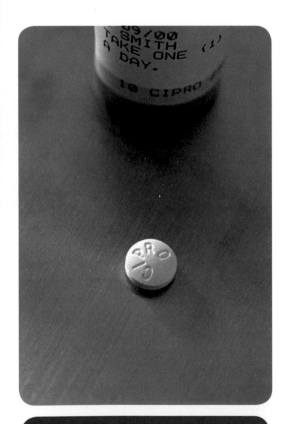

There are many different antibiot-ics used to treat UTIs. Doctors can determine the appropriate one for each patient.

ANTIBIOTICS

The word "antibiotic" comes from the Greek word *antibiosis*, or "against life." Antibiotics are medications used to destroy or slow down the growth of bacteria. The first antibiotic was penicillin. It was first put to use by Alexander Fleming in 1928. Later developments led to the effective use of antibiotics on the battlefields of World War II, saving many lives. The drugs have cured infections such as tuberculosis, pneumonia, and whooping cough. These infections used to cause millions of deaths each year. Doctors are now concerned that if antibiotics are overused, there is a risk that some bacteria will become resistant, meaning the antibiotic becomes less effective against a particular type of bacterium.

TREATING YOUR UTI

In addition to taking your antibiotics, there are many things you can do at home to help your body recover from your UTI. First, most medical professionals suggest that you drink a lot of water to flush out the bacteria. You need to allow your body to rest. It is a good idea to stop playing sports and engaging in any vigorous exercise for a few days. Sleep allows your body to recover. Since you are not

Drinking a lot of water can help flush bacteria out of the bladder. The right amount of water will produce urine that is light yellow.

contagious, you don't need to stay home from school unless you are in too much pain to concentrate or are going to the bathroom too much.

Make sure to eat a healthy diet while treating your UTI. There are some drinks that may irritate your bladder and cause pain on urination. Avoid coffee, alcohol, and soft drinks that contain citrus juices and caffeine. A warm heating pad on your abdomen will make you feel better. Make a follow-up visit to the doctor if you don't start feeling better within three or four days.

While most often not serious, UTIs cause millions of dollars in lost work days for working women and teens and thousands of hours of lost instruction time for students each year. Antibiotics have proven to be a quick, safe, and effective treatment for patients who use them correctly. UTI sufferers need to follow their doctors' instructions. They also

UTIs AND YEAST INFECTIONS

While treating a UTI with antibiotics, some women will develop a yeast infection. Antibiotics, by killing off bacteria, change the normal pH, or acidity level, in the vagina. A yeast infection is caused by a fungus called candida. Candida lives in the vagina in small amounts. When the pH changes, the yeast can grow and multiply. Symptoms of a yeast infection include vaginal itching and irritation and a cottage cheese–like discharge. Yeast infections can be treated by anti-fungal creams, ointments, tablets, or suppositories. The medications are available over the counter at most pharmacies. If the treatment doesn't clear up the infection, you need to let your doctor know. Some women claim that eating yogurt or taking acidophilus pills prevents yeast infections while they are on antibiotics. Researchers as yet have not come to any conclusions and say more studies are needed.

need to rest and take care of themselves at home. With proper treatment, someone with a UTI can be up and back to regular activity within a few days.

MYTHS AND FACTS

MYTH
Drinking cranberry juice will cure a UTI.

FACT
Cranberries contain hippuric acid, which helps prevent bacteria from attaching to the urethra. They can help some people from getting a UTI but do nothing to cure one.

MYTH
You can get a UTI from a dirty toilet.

FACT
UTIs are not contagious. You cannot get them from a dirty toilet seat or any other surface.

MYTH
Only women get UTIs.

FACT
Although women get 80 percent of all UTIs, men can get a bladder infection. It is more common in older men, who have more risk factors.

CHAPTER THREE

How to Prevent UTIs

U rinary tract infections can be treated effectively by taking a course of antibiotics. However, before they can get to a doctor and pharmacy, most UTI sufferers endure several days of painful and inconvenient symptoms. The ideal situation would be to prevent UTIs from occurring. There are many strategies you can employ to reduce the chances that you will get a UTI.

HYGIENE PRACTICES

Like most teens, you probably learned basic hygiene practices at home from your parents. You also received lessons on how to prevent illness and infection at school in health, physical education (PE), and sex education classes. UTIs, however, involve topics that many parents and teachers are reluctant to discuss: bathroom

Though the topics might be embarrassing, most teens will find that parents can be a great source of information about health and infections.

procedures and sex. Toddlers are taught how to wipe themselves after a bowel movement. Then the topic is usually not brought up again. Parents might teach their teens how to protect against pregnancy and sexually transmitted diseases (STDs). Few parents remind their daughters to use the bathroom before and after sex. Teens most often learn how to prevent UTIs after they have had one.

The most effective way to avoid getting a UTI is to prevent bacteria from getting near your vagina and urethra. Proper wiping from the front of the genital area to back is essential, as bacteria from the rectum is the main cause of UTIs. During their monthly period, girls need to replace tampons and pads often, at least every couple of hours, to avoid a buildup of bacteria. Doctors recommend that you drink a lot of water to flush any bacteria out of your bladder. The most common way of measuring if you are drinking enough is that your pee stays a pale yellow color. If it is dark yellow, you are not drinking enough water.

Going to the bathroom often is an important strategy for preventing UTIs. There are many reasons why some people wait to urinate. They may be working hard on a project. The bathroom may be in an inconvenient location. Students may be discouraged from asking for a restroom pass because it is a distraction in class. You may find yourself trying to hold your urine because you don't want to interrupt a movie, miss a play in a game, or wait in a long restroom line. The longer the urine is in your bladder, the easier it is for bacteria to multiply. Health professionals encourage everyone to empty their bladders at least every few hours. If you are drinking as much water as you should be, you should be ready to visit the restroom that often.

You may enjoy soaking in a bubble bath as a way of relaxing tired and tense muscles at the end of a long day. Doctors encourage women, especially those prone to UTIs, to shower

To avoid UTIs, showers are preferable to baths, as soaking in bubbles and bath salts can irritate the genital area.

instead of taking baths. Women should at least avoid the soap or bath salts used to produce the bubbles and fragrance in a bath. Substances in the bubble mixture can irritate the urethra. This irritation can cause a burning sensation during urination. This pain may cause you to avoid going to the bathroom, or when you do, wiping quickly or incompletely.

There was a time, in the mid-twentieth century, when women thought douching was part of good daily hygiene. Douching is cleansing the vagina by squirting a solution of water, deodorizing chemicals, and soap into the vagina. Medical professionals now have numerous studies that show that douching upsets the natural chemical and bacterial balance of the vagina. The solutions kill off beneficial bacteria, allowing bad bacteria, such as *E. coli*, to grow. The bad bacteria can easily be pushed into the urethra, causing a UTI. Healthy vaginas have natural processes that keep them clean. Vaginal odor is also normal. Sprays used to deodorize the vaginal area can cause the same sort of irritation caused by bubble baths. Doctors advise using mild soaps and body washes in a daily shower to keep the vaginal area clean.

THE BENEFITS OF PROPER NUTRITION

Women have known for many years that cranberry juice can help prevent UTIs. Cranberries contain a type of acid that seems to prevent bacteria from attaching to the urethra. Cranberries are very tart, so sugar is added to most commercial cranberry juice. Sugar, however, is not helpful for people with UTIs. If you want to drink cranberry juice to prevent UTIs, drink it unsweetened or look for cranberry supplements in tablet form. Cranberry juice cannot cure a UTI.

Most health care providers advise teens and young adults to follow recommended guidelines for staying healthy. Dr. Elizabeth Kavaler, a urologist in New York City, says in a 2012 HealthDay article, "The best defense against

A nutritious diet full of healthy fruits and vegetables helps teen bodies build up immunities against infections.

urinary tract infections is to exercise, eat well and get proper sleep so your immune system is strong and can fend off what you can't see, including *E. coli.*" For most women, nutritional supplements aren't necessary to help a healthy immune system fight off invaders.

HOW TO PREVENT UTIs IF YOU ARE SEXUALLY ACTIVE

The strongest risk factor for UTIs in teens and young adults is the frequency of sex. According to a 2013 report by the *New York Times*, "nearly 80% of all urinary tract infections in [young] women occur within 24 hours of intercourse." If you are sexually active, reducing the amount of sex will reduce your risk of getting a UTI. The article reports that very few celibate women get UTIs.

Changing your form of contraceptive can reduce your risk of getting a UTI. Diaphragms can bruise the area near the bladder, making

DOES MY UNDERWEAR MAKE A DIFFERENCE?

Health care professionals have long advised that women who are prone to UTIs wear cotton underwear. Nylon underwear traps moisture near your body, especially when it's hot outside. Bacteria love to grow in warm, moist places. Many women think they are safe with just cotton crotches on their underwear. However, any fabric that is non-breathable near the vagina or urethra will trap moisture. Thongs also put women at increased risk, regardless of the fabric. The skinny shape leaves the vulva more exposed to whatever they are wearing, such as Lycra or spandex leggings. The thin band tends to move around, possibly transferring bacteria from one spot to another. Bikini underwear is a better choice for women who like a minimal look.

it susceptible to bacteria. Spermicidal foams or gels, whether used with a diaphragm or on their own as a contraceptive, are also associated with increased risk of UTIs. If you use these forms of contraceptives and you have had a UTI, you need to discuss with your health care provider other forms of contraceptives you can use.

Most doctors recommend some urinary habits to reduce UTIs in sexually active women. Urinating before having sex reduces the amount of urine that can be infected by bacteria. Going to the bathroom right after having sex can flush out bacteria before it has a chance to establish itself in the urethra and bladder. It is also a good idea to clean your genital area with a mild soap and water after having sex.

WHAT TO DO IF YOU GET FREQUENT UTIs

Some people, mostly women, get one or two UTIs every year. If you get more than one UTI a year, your doctor may take several steps to treat you. First, he or she may determine exactly which antibiotic to prescribe. One way to do this is to culture your urine. Usually to diagnose a UTI, a doctor or nurse will dip a stick into your urine to detect nitrates or white blood cells, which signal a UTI. A culture is done by putting some of your urine into a dish with a substance that encourages any bacteria to grow. Then the bacteria can be identified and a specific antibiotic prescribed. You might be asked to take the antibiotic for longer than a week.

Your health care provider might want to see if your urinary tract is normal. There are several tests that can be done. One is a kidney and bladder ultrasound. A radiology technician will use a device called a transducer to bounce painless sound waves off your organs to create an image of their structure. This procedure is done in the doctor's office or an outpatient center. The images can show abnormalities in the organs.

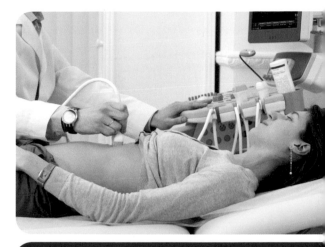

To help determine the cause of frequent UTIs, a physician might order an ultrasound to look for organ abnormalities.

A voiding cysto-urethrogram is an X-ray image of your bladder and urethra taken while your bladder is full. Your bladder will be filled with a special dye to make your organs clearly visible on the X-ray. Then you will be asked to urinate into a container. The radiologist can see how your bladder works and if the flow of urine is normal.

Other tests that might be done are computerized tomography (CT) scans, magnetic resonance imaging (MRI), radionuclide scans, and urodynamics testing. These tests can find abnormalities and other problems that might provide reasons for your UTIs. You might be referred to a urologist, a doctor who specializes in diseases and conditions of the urinary tract. While medication cures most urinary tract infections, you might need surgery to correct a condition that may continue to give you UTIs if you don't address the underlying problem. For instance, surgery might be necessary if there is tissue that obstructs the urethra.

For some patients who get recurrent UTIs, a doctor might prescribe antibiotics as UTI prevention as well as treatment. For instance, a woman might take a one-dose antibiotic after having sex. Some women might be prescribed a continual low dose of antibiotics as a way of preventing UTIs. These therapies have side effects. Some women might develop resistance to particular antibiotics if they take them for long periods of time. Other women might develop yeast infections.

Most women who get a UTI will learn the strategies that are effective in preventing them. Some women, and possibly some men, will get recurrent UTIs. They will need to work as a team with their health care providers. The right antibiotic for their particular strains of bacteria, plus their own nutritional and behavioral practices, can go a long way in solving their UTI issues.

CHAPTER FOUR

Complications with UTIs

People suffered from urinary tract infections long before doctors figured out ways to cure their ailments. An ancient Egyptian papyrus recommended herbal treatments for urinary problems. The Greek physician Hippocrates thought that urinary pain was caused by disharmony in the body. Roman and Arab physicians expanded knowledge about urinary issues. However, UTIs weren't effectively diagnosed or treated until the discovery that microorganisms caused disease in the nineteenth century. This discovery stimulated more advances in the treatment of UTIs in the twentieth century than had occurred in the previous five centuries.

Now there are more ways to diagnose and treat UTIs than ever. Over-the-counter home self-test kits are available to diagnose your own UTIs. There have been huge advances in imaging technology, such as X-rays, ultrasounds, nuclear imaging, and MRIs. New antibiotics have been developed that are safer and more effective than older medications. Physicians are finding ways to more accurately match a person's particular strain of bacteria with an antibiotic that specifically targets it. Researchers are experimenting with vaccines in the form of nasal sprays to prevent UTIs. However, problems with the treatment of UTIs are a big concern to health care professionals.

WHAT CAN GO WRONG

Most UTIs will clear up with antibiotics and a healthy lifestyle. Occasionally a UTI patient will develop complications that can become serious if not treated. Complications are more likely in people with preexisting health conditions, such as diabetes or a weakened immune system. Pregnant women sometimes develop complications. If you don't get better when the doctor predicted, you need to make a follow-up appointment to see what is wrong.

Men who are being treated for a UTI are at risk for complications that affect the prostate. The prostate is a walnut-size gland that secretes the fluid that makes up semen. A UTI can spread infection to the prostate, causing prostatitis. This condition can be treated by antibiotics.

Because the kidneys are near the bladder, bacteria can travel from the bladder to the kidneys. The symptoms of a kidney infection develop quickly. You might feel pain in your side, in your lower back, and around your genitals. You may develop a fever and chills. You will generally feel tired, weak, and sick. You will probably lose your appetite and may develop diarrhea.

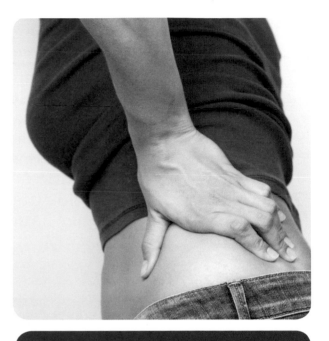

Fever, nausea, and back and side pain are all signs that a UTI has progressed into a kidney infection.

Your doctor will most likely prescribe more antibiotics and then schedule a follow-up visit in about two weeks. This is the length of time for a kidney infection to be resolved. Getting a lot of rest and drinking a lot of fluids will help you feel better. While you have a fever, it is best to stay home from school. You are not contagious, but you probably won't feel like concentrating on learning.

Very rarely, a UTI can be the source of a life-threatening illness. Some bacteria are hard to eliminate because they have become resistant to most common antibiotics. A kidney infection that is resistant to antibiotics can lead to a condition called sepsis. Bacteria get into the blood, which triggers the immune system to release chemicals into the blood. The inflammation that results from these chemicals can lead to organ failure. This is what happened to a twenty-year-old Brazilian model. In 2009, Mariana Bridi contracted a UTI that was resistant to antibiotics. The illness progressed to a kidney infection and then to sepsis. Doctors amputated her hands and feet because of

RESPONSIBLE ANTIBIOTIC USE

The CDC has many recommendations about responsible antibiotic use. The agency asks that you use antibiotics only when they are likely to be beneficial. The CDC also recommends that you follow your doctor's instructions exactly. Do not stop taking the pills before you run out, even if you are feeling better. If you stop too soon, some bacteria may survive. Don't take antibiotics prescribed for someone else or those that have been prescribed for another illness. Taking the wrong medicine can delay treatment and allow bacteria to multiply. If you get a nonbacterial infection, such as the flu, ask your doctor how you can feel better without antibiotics.

lack of circulation. Eventually she died from complications of the infection.

ANTIBIOTIC RESISTANCE

One problem in the treatment of all bacterial infections is antibiotic resistance. Since antibiotics were developed seventy years ago, these drugs have greatly reduced illness and death from infectious diseases. However, the drugs have been used so widely that the bacteria the antibiotics have been developed to kill have adapted to them. The bacteria changes in some way. These changes reduce or eliminate the effectiveness of the drugs that are made to cure the diseases. According to the CDC, at least two million people in the United States become infected with bacteria that are resistant to antibiotics. At least twenty-three thousand people die each year from these infections. Many more die from other conditions that were complicated by an antibiotic-resistant infection. Some examples of these infections include pneumonia, sexually transmitted diseases, and skin diseases.

It is not just the United States that is battling this problem. Antibiotic resistance occurs everywhere in the world. The CDC calls it one of the world's most pressing public health problems. The effects are devastating. People who have infections caused by drug-resistant bacteria are likely to have longer and more expensive hospital stays.

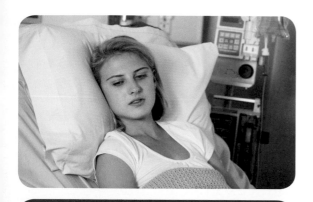

When antibiotics don't work because bacteria is resistant to them, patients suffer from longer and more complicated illnesses.

When the drug that is treating their infection doesn't work, patients require treatment with drugs that may be less effective, more toxic, and more expensive. These patients may suffer more and pay more for treatment. The patients also may spread their disease to family members, friends, and coworkers.

There are many causes of antibiotic resistance. One is the routine use of antibiotics in food-producing animals such as poultry and cattle. The bacteria in the animals develop resistance. Consumers then pick up the bacteria either in the preparation or the eating of the animals. Another cause is the use of antibiotics to treat viral infections. Too many people demand antibiotics from their doctors when they have viral infections, such as a cold. Antibiotics cannot stop

Some food-producing animals are given low doses of antibiotics over a long period of time to help them grow larger. This may result in bacteria that are resistant.

UROLOGY: A HOT MEDICAL FIELD

A urologist is a doctor who specializes in diseases of the urinary tract and male reproductive organs. Urologists complete a rigorous training period after medical school of at least five years. They use fiber-optic equipment, lasers, and robotics in treating diseases and disorders such as cancer, incontinence, and kidney stones. Urologists are predicted to be one of the most-sought medical specialists in the next decade.

or prevent an infection caused by a virus. The CDC is currently studying the impact of widespread use of antibacterial soaps and solutions. Antibacterial products are essential in health care settings. However, there may be a link between the widespread use of these products and an increase in antibiotic resistance.

10 GREAT QUESTIONS
TO ASK A DOCTOR

1. Can I spread my UTI to my boyfriend if we have sex?

2. Why do I keep getting UTIs?

3. Why does my UTI not clear up after I take an antibiotic?

4. What would happen if I tried to heal myself and did not see a doctor?

5. Can a UTI affect my period?

6. Can I use leftover antibiotics from another infection?

7. Can my family members get my UTI?

8. Will cranberry juice cure my UTI?

9. Can a person die from a UTI?

10. How can I prevent a yeast infection while taking antibiotics?

CHAPTER FIVE

Coping with a UTI

Like most teens, you probably hate being sick. You have a busy life with a lot of activities. You want to keep up with school, sports, friends, clubs, jobs, and volunteer work. You can't afford to take time off to take care of a UTI. However, part of the process of becoming an adult is taking responsibility for your health. This means following your doctor's orders, learning as much as you can about your infection, taking advantage of resources that are available to you, and managing your emotional responses. UTIs don't just impact your physical health. You need to also pay attention to your mental and emotional well-being.

Your doctor probably gave you a list of dos and don'ts in recovering from a UTI. You were probably told to rest until you no longer have a fever and your temperature returns to normal. Resting gives your immune system a chance to fight the infection. A fever is a sign that white blood cells have arrived in your bladder to kill the bacteria. The body raises the heat level to stimulate the white blood cells and inhibit the growth of bacteria. A decreasing fever is a sign that the white blood cells have done their job. If you are taking antibiotics, it shouldn't take more than a day or two at home to start feeling a lot better.

When you do return to physical activity, you need to take some precautions. If your clothing gets sweaty, change it immediately. Use the bathroom before and right after sports or PE classes. Drink a lot of water, more than usual. Do everything you can to minimize the chances that bacteria can get near your urethra.

After a UTI, you should wait to return to physical activity until your fever and symptoms are gone and your energy has returned.

LEARNING ABOUT YOUR UTI

Learning about your body and the ways it responds to disease is a great step toward responsible adulthood. There are many ways to access reliable health information. The first place is your doctor's office or family health clinic. Your health professionals may have informational handouts or bro-chures on UTIs that you can take home with you to read. They also may refer you to resources that will answer your questions.

Your health insurance com-pany is another good place to find information. Many companies have extensive websites filled with repu-table facts and suggestions for treating your UTI. Some have nurse hotlines that you can call to discuss your questions.

Health care professionals in your doctor's office can be a great resource in learning about preventing infections. They may wait for you to ask questions, though.

Other companies may have chat features on their websites. You may need your insurance identification number to access these features.

Libraries are good places for reference materials. Most public libraries have online databases that are available to anyone with a library card. The reference librarian at your local library branch can show you how to use these databases. Many schools provide databases for their students to use for research. All of these databases are likely to have current information on health topics.

Teens today are used to researching most any topic on the Internet. Doing a search, however, may bring up hits for websites that do not provide reliable information. Anyone can create a website that popularizes a health topic, regardless of the accuracy of the information. There are vendors who want to sell products but don't offer clinical proof that they work. There are believers in health philosophies that have no basis in science. How can you find reliable, easily understandable information that can provide the facts you need about your UTI? Here are some tips for locating trustworthy medical information on the Internet.

- The U.S. government provides health and medical information for consumers. The U.S. National Library of Medicine and the National Institutes of Health sponsor the MedlinePlus websites. There are more than eight hundred topics explained in English and Spanish. For government websites, look for a .gov in the address.

- Reputable hospitals make available, through their websites, trustworthy health and medical information. One of the largest hospitals is the Mayo Clinic. Through MayoClinic.com, thousands of physicians and researchers provide in-depth information on hundreds of diseases and conditions.
- Disease-specific organizations offer websites dedicated to informing consumers about their particular disease. For instance, the National Institute of Diabetes and Digestive and Kidney Diseases provides the National Kidney and Urologic Diseases Information Clearinghouse (NKUDIC). This well-organized website offers a wealth of information about UTIs.

SUPPORTING A FRIEND OR FAMILY MEMBER WHO HAS A UTI

Teens with urinary tract infections may be reluctant to tell family and friends about their condition. It is awkward to discuss a disease, especially one connected to such a taboo topic as urinating. Once you do share the news, you will find that it feels good to have their support.

FORMING A GOOD RELATIONSHIP WITH YOUR DOCTOR

Pediatricians and family doctors can be your biggest allies in navigating through the health issues of adolescence and young adulthood. They have a lot of experience helping teens with questions about substance abuse, sexually transmitted diseases, and mental health issues. But they need help from you. To accurately diagnose and treat an illness or condition, they need you to be completely honest. It may be difficult to admit that you are sexually active to a doctor who has been treating you since you were a baby. Your physician isn't there to judge you. Taking responsibility for your most accurate information possible about you.

If you have done your research and have accurate information at your fingertips, you can dispel any misconceptions family and friends may have about UTIs. From you, they can learn that the condition is not contagious, it is easily treated, and it sometimes, but not always results, from sexual activity. They can even cover for you if acquaintances notice you disappearing to the restroom often.

If someone you know contracts a UTI, you can be a great support to her. Showing empathy for her pain and discomfort is usually appreciated. You might have to explain her condition to others in a sensitive way. The sick person may be feeling embarrassed or guilty that she caused her own illness. If you know the facts about UTIs, you can lead the ill friend to realize that she has the power to prevent future UTIs. Encouraging her to rest, drink water, pay attention to nutrition, and take medicine regularly are all ways to show support.

If you have a UTI and are in an intimate relationship with someone, honest communication about your condition is essential. Your partner needs to know all the facts about what causes UTIs and how they can be prevented. He or she needs to understand the connection between some forms of contraceptives and UTIs. Together you might need to research alternate forms of birth control. It will be uncomfortable to have sex while treating a UTI. It is a good idea to take a break from sexual

You can support a friend with a UTI by providing accurate information and advice, as well as sympathy.

activity while treating the condition. A support-ive partner will want to do everything possible to keep the other partner healthy and positive.

TELLING THE APPROPRIATE PEOPLE

As a teen, much of your day is spent at school. Attending classes and extracurricular activities will be difficult if you are having symptoms of a UTI, such as needing to go to the bathroom often and feeling pain in your pelvic area. Let-ting the appropriate people know about your UTI will make your day go more smoothly. Either you or a parent should first notify the school nurse or nurse's aide that you are being treated for a UTI. School nurses cannot diag-nose or prescribe medications for a UTI. However, they can work with you and your teachers to make sure your needs are met.

Either you or a parent needs to notify your teachers about your UTI. You most likely won't be attending school while your symptoms are at their worst and you still have a fever and pain. When you return to school, however, you still might have to get quickly to a restroom or go lie down for a few minutes. Supportive teachers who know about your UTI can issue a pass to the restroom or nurse's office without a lot of attention and embarrassment. After you return to school, you still might need a day or two of recovery before you participate in PE classes or sports. Make sure you keep your

While it is best to be completely honest with your coaches, you can also just tell them that you have an infection and need to take it easy for a few days.

coaches in the loop. They will not want you back to practice until you are completely recovered.

If you have a job, you do not have to be more specific when you call in than "I'm not feeling well enough to work so I'm staying home today." Employers will not want you working if you are not at your best. They will appreciate as much notice as possible so they can arrange a replacement for you. Make sure that you do the calling, not a parent. You might need to bring an excuse from your doctor if you are out more than a day or two.

For some teens, the worst part of having UTIs is telling others that they have one. It is not a topic a lot of teens know about, and what they do know is often inaccurate. If you are prepared to answer questions, you will find that most of your friends will want to know what you have learned about UTIs. Acquaintances, teachers, coaches, and school personnel will likely be sympathetic and nonjudgmental. They will want you to focus on recovery. Adults will realize that once someone suffers through a UTI, he or she will do everything possible to avoid getting another one.

There are many challenges in the treatment of urinary tract infections for both health care professionals and patients. Doctors have to make decisions about prescribing antibiotics. Patients need to learn about their infections so they can treat themselves effectively and prevent themselves from getting another infection. If you or someone you know has a UTI, your best weapon against this disease is knowledge. Becoming an adult means assuming responsibility for maintaining the health of your body. You can meet this challenge by learning about infections and diseases and what causes them. Once you have the knowledge you need, you can make the right choices to continue living a healthy, responsible lifestyle.

GLOSSARY

celibate Abstaining from sexual relations.

compromised Unable to function well because of disease or side effects of a treatment.

contaminated Made impure or unsuitable by contact with something not clean.

cystitis Swelling and pain of the bladder due to bacterial infection.

database A collection of related data organized for convenient access.

diabetes A disorder in which the body does not produce enough insulin.

diaphragm A domed rubber device placed over the cervix to prevent conception.

diverticula Sacs that branch off from canals or cavities.

douche A method of cleaning the vagina with a solution of vinegar and water.

inflammation Swelling and pain as a reaction of tissues to bacteria.

insulin A hormone that regulates the metabolism of glucose.

microbe An organism too small to be seen by the unaided eye.

pneumonia A disease of the lungs, caused by bacteria.

pyelonephritis Inflammation of the kidney, caused by a bacterial infection.

recurrence The return of a previous condition.

sepsis An invasion of the body by microorganisms or their toxins.

spermicide A sperm-killing preparation to prevent pregnancy.

stagnant Stale or foul from standing, as a pool of water.

symptom A sign that shows evidence of a disease or disorder.

toxin Any poison produced by an organism, such as bacteria.

urethra The tube that carries urine from the bladder out of the body.

virus A microscopic agent that causes infection in cells.

FOR MORE INFORMATION

Advocates for Youth
2000 M Street NW, Suite 750
Washington, DC 20036
(202) 419-3420
Website: http://www.advocatesforyouth.org
Advocates for Youth helps young people make
   responsible decisions about their reproductive and sexual health.

Canadian Women's Health Network
Suite 203, 419 Graham Avenue
Winnipeg, MB R3C 0M3
Canada
(204) 942-5500
Website: http://www.cwhn.ca/en
This organization is dedicated to improving
   the health and lives of girls and women in
   Canada.

Healthy Teen Network
1501 Saint Paul Street, Suite 124
Baltimore, MD 21202
(410) 685-0410
Website: http://www.healthyteennetwork.org
This organization supports and empowers
   teens to lead healthy sexual, reproductive,
   and family lives.

Office on Women's Health
U.S. Department of Health and Human Services
200 Independence Avenue SW
Washington, DC 20201

(800) 994-9662
Website: http://www.womenshealth.gov
This organization provides national leadership
    and coordination to improve the health of
    girls and women through policy, education,
    and model programs.

Women's Health Matters
Women's College Hospital
76 Grenville Street, Room 6153
Toronto, ON M5S 1B2
Canada
(416) 323-6400
Website: http://www.womenshealthmatters.ca
This organization provides information on
    women's health from the Women's College
    Hospital in Toronto, Ontario.

WEBSITES

Because of the changing nature of Internet
links, Rosen Publishing has developed an online
list of websites related to the subject of this
book. This site is updated regularly. Please use
this link to access the list:

http://www.rosenlinks.com/YSH/UTI

FOR FURTHER READING

The Boston Women's Health Book Collective. *Our Bodies, Ourselves.* New York, NY: Touchstone, 2011.

Feinstein, Stephen. *Sexuality and Teens: What You Should Know About Sex, Abstinence, Birth Control, Pregnancy, and STDs* (Issues in Focus Today). Berkeley Heights, NJ: Enslow Publishers, 2009.

Fonda, Jane. *Being a Teen: Everything Teen Girls & Boys Should Know About Relationships, Sex, Love, Health, Identity & More.* New York, NY: Random House, 2014.

Hasler, Nikol. *Sex: A Book for Teens: An Uncensored Guide to Your Body, Sex, and Safety.* San Francisco, CA: Zest Books, 2010.

Henderson, Elisabeth. *100 Questions You'd Never Ask Your Parents: Straight Answers to Teens' Questions About Sex, Sexuality, and Health.* Revised edition. New York, NY: Roaring Brook Press, 2013.

Mayo Clinic. *Mayo Clinic Family Health Book.* New York, NY: Time Inc. Home Entertainment, 2009.

Roizen, Michael, and Mehmet Oz. *YOU: The Owner's Manual for Teens: A Guide to a Healthy Body and Happy Life.* New York, NY: Free Press, 2011.

Vincent, Beverly, and Robert Greenberger. *Frequently Asked Questions About Birth Control.* (FAQ: Teen Life). New York, NY: Rosen Publishing Group, 2011.

BIBLIOGRAPHY

Alexander, Linda, Judith LaRosa, Helaine Bader, Susan Garfield, and William Alexander. *New Dimensions in Women's Health.* Burlington, MA: Jones & Bartlett Learning, 2014.

Brusch, John. "Catheter-Related Urinary Tract Infection." January 8, 2013. Medscape. Retrieved September 21, 2014 (http:// emedicine.medscape.com/article/2040035 -overview#aw2aab6b3).

Centers for Disease Control and Prevention. "Antibiotic/Antimicrobial Resistance." August 6, 2014. Retrieved October 5, 2014 (http:// www.cdc.gov/drugresistance).

Cleveland Clinic. "Hold the Cranberries—UTI Myths Explained." December 4, 2013. Retrieved October 10, 2014 (http://health .clevelandclinic.org/2013/12/hold-the -cranberries-uti-myths-explained).

FoxNews. "Model Dies After Losing Hands, Feet to Urinary Tract Infection." January 24, 2009. Retrieved October 8, 2014 (http://www .foxnews.com/story/2009/01/24/model -dies-after-losing-hands-feet-to-urinary-tract -infection).

Gallagher, Jason, and Conan MacDougall. *Antibiotics Simplified.* Burlington, MA: Jones & Bartlett Learning, 2014.

Hudson, Tori. *Women's Encyclopedia of Natural Medicine.* New York, NY: McGraw-Hill, 2007.

Kodner, Charles, and Thomas Gupton. "Recurrent Urinary Tract Infections in Women: Diagnosis and Management." *American*

Family Physician, September 15, 2010. Retrieved October 8, 2014 (http://www.ncbi .nlm.nih.gov/pubmed?term=Thomas%20 Gupton%20EK%5BAuthor%5D&cauthor=true &cauthor_uid=20842992).

Krupnick, Ellie, and Rebecca Adams. "Why Your Thong May Be Bad for Your Health." Huffington Post, October 15, 2013. Retrieved October 1, 2014 (http://www .huffingtonpost.com/2013/10/15/thong -health_n_4026307.html).

Mann, Denise. "E. Coli in Chicken Linked to Urinary Tract Infections." HealthDay, February 12, 2012. Retrieved October 7, 2014 (http:// consumer.healthday.com/vitamins-and -nutritional-information-27/food-and -nutrition-news-316/e-coli-in-chicken-linked -to-urinary-tract-infections-661775.html).

Mayo Clinic. "Urinary Tract Infection (UTI)." August 29, 2012. Retrieved October 8, 2014 (http://www.mayoclinic.org/diseases -conditions/urinary-tract-infection/basics /treatment/con-20037892).

McKenna, Maryn. "Antibiotic Resistance: The Last Resort." Nature.com, July 24, 2013. Retrieved October 10, 2014 (http://www .nature.com/news/antibiotic-resistance -the-last-resort-1.13426).

National Kidney and Urologic Diseases Information Clearinghouse (NKUDIC). "What I Need to Know About Urinary Tract Infections." December 2011. Retrieved September 21, 2014 (http://kidney.niddk.nih.gov/kudiseases /pubs/uti_ez/v).

New York Times. "Urinary Tract Infection— Adults." September 17, 2013. Retrieved October 10, 2014 (http://www.nytimes.com /health/guides/disease/urinary-tract -infection/risk-factors.html).

Nickel, J. C. "Management of Urinary Tract Infections: Historical Perspective and Current Strategies: Part 1—Before Antibiotics." *Journal of Urology*, January 2005. Retrieved October 2, 2014 (http://www.ncbi.nlm.nih.gov /pubmed?term=Nickel%20JC%5BAuthor%5 D&cauthor=true&cauthor_uid=15592018).

Rose, Angela. "There's No Shortage of Physician Jobs in the U.S. but Certain Specialties Top the Recruitment and Hiring Demand List." HealtheCareers.com, November 19, 2013. Retrieved October 8, 2014 (http://www .healthecareers.com/article/top-specialties -with-the-highest-hiring-demand/173862).

Sabatine, Marc. *Pocket Medicine: The Massachusetts General Hospital Handbook of Internal Medicine.* Philadelphia, PA: Lippincott Williams & Wilkins, 2014.

Scarleteen. "An Infection Getting Worse and Worse: Can I Just Wait It Out?" May 2, 2013. Retrieved September 21, 2014 (http://www .scarleteen.com/article/advice/an_infection _getting_worse_and_worse_can_i_just_wait_it _out).

Stein, Jill. "Urinary Tract Infections More Com-
    mon in Diabetics." *Renal & Urology News*, July
    8, 2013. Retrieved October 10, 2014 (http://
    www.renalandurologynews.com/urinary-tract
    -infections-more-common-in-diabetics/article
    /302056).
TeensHealth. "Urinary Tract Infections." January
    2012. Retrieved September 21, 2014 (http://
    kidshealth.org/teen/sexual_health/stds/uti
    .html?tracking=T_RelatedArticle#).
Womenshealth.gov. "Vaginal Yeast Infections Fact
    Sheet." July 16, 2012. Retrieved October 8,
    2014 (http://www.womenshealth.gov
    /publications/our-publications/fact-sheet
    /vaginal-yeast-infections.html).

INDEX

A

antibiotics, 6, 18, 19–20, 21, 22, 23, 25, 32, 34, 35–36, 37–38, 42, 44, 52
   antibiotic resistance, 39–41
anus, 8, 9

B

bacteria, 6, 8, 9, 10–11, 12, 14, 15, 18, 19, 20, 21, 23, 24, 26–27, 29, 30–31, 32, 34, 36, 37, 38, 39, 40, 43–44
bacterial infections, 18, 39
bladder, 7, 8, 9, 11, 12, 14–15, 17, 18, 20, 22, 27, 30–31, 32, 33, 36, 43–44
   bladder infections, 11, 18, 24
blood, 7, 14, 18, 38
burning sensation, 4, 9–10, 17, 28

C

complications, 35–41
contraceptives, 12, 30, 31, 49
cranberry juice, 24, 29, 42
cystitis, 6, 11

D

deaths, 10, 21, 39
diabetes, 14, 36
diaphragms, 12, 30–31
diarrhea, 10, 37
douching, 28–29

E

E. coli, 10, 11, 29, 30
exercise, 21, 29–30

F

fever, 11, 18, 37, 43–44, 50

H

hygiene, 25–29

I

immune systems, 15, 29–30, 36, 38, 43

K

kidney infection, 6, 11, 19, 36–38
kidneys, 7, 10, 14–15, 36

N

National Kidney and Urologic Diseases Information Clearinghouse (NKUDIC), 4, 47
nutrition, 29–30, 34

P

pain, 11, 15, 17, 20, 21–22, 25, 28, 35, 37, 48–49, 50
pregnant women, 15, 36

ABOUT THE AUTHOR

As a high school and college educator for over thirty years, Susan Henneberg has taught thousands of teens and young adults about the responsibilities of adulthood. She is the author of numerous books on such topics as teen health, social media, career planning, and academic and personal success. She is a parent of three daughters and lives in Reno, Nevada.

PHOTO CREDITS